The Formentera Guide

ISBN: 978-0-557-33679-1

Index

1. Introduction

Formentera is one of the last true paradises in the Mediterranean, but rather than wax lyrical about turquoise seas and white sand beaches I have tried to make this guide as practical as possible to help you make the most of your stay. There are plenty of photos included in the guide, and the natural beauty of the island speaks for itself.

Formentera is the smallest of the Balearic Islands, and with an area of 32 square miles (83 sq km), and length of 12 miles (20km), it's easy to explore.

Although the island is just two nautical miles south of Ibiza, the distance between the two ports is 12 miles, and the journey takes around 30 minutes by ferry. The permanent population is around 9,500, but the summer months see nearly half a million tourists come and go.

Despite the number of visitors the island has done a great job of preserving its natural beauty through a number of initiatives, including a dune regeneration program, resistance to tarmac on the roads, building restrictions, and encouraging tourists to use bikes. Even though Formentera is next to the booming party destination of Ibiza, and the major tourist island of Mallorca, it feels like a remote destination. Without an airport it takes that extra effort to get there, and this has helped the island to maintain its heritage.

If you have any comments on the book, or want to get in touch on any other matter, then please just email us at admin @formenteraguide.com

Have a great holiday!

1.1.   Geography

The geography of the island is unusual: it is mostly flat except for the plateaus of la Mola in the east, and Cap de Barbaria in the south. The narrow isthmus known as Es Carnatge connects these two. There is also a northern peninsula of beaches and dunes known as Es Trucadors.

Because of its shape, with two bulbous plateaus joined by a long isthmus, Formentera has a relatively long coastline. Even in peak season you should be able to find secluded beaches away from the tourist throng.

La Mola Road (PM 820) is the main artery of the island running from the north-western port of La Savina down to the south-eastern village El Pilar de la Mola. However, if you are travelling by bicycle then there is a network of paths behind the highway that are far more scenic.

The following table gives you a sense of the distances involved.

Formentera Distances

Distance (kilometers)														
	Cala en Baster	Cala Saona	Ca Mari	Cap de Barbaria	Es Calo	Es Mal Pas	Es Pujols	Es Arenals	La Mola	La Savina	Porto Sale	Punta Prima	Sant Ferran	Sant Francesc	Es Far de la Mola
Cala en Baster	-	10	4	14	8	9	4	10	14	8	9	4	2	5	16
Cala Saona	10	-	11	9	14	8	10	16	20	8	9	10	8	5	22
Ca Mari	4	11	-	15	7	10	5	9	13	9	10	5	3	6	15
Cap de Barbaria	14	9	15	-	18	12	14	20	24	12	13	14	12	9	26
Es Calo	8	14	7	18	-	13	8	2	6	12	13	8	6	9	8
Es Mal Pas	9	8	10	12	13	-	9	15	19	7	8	9	7	4	21
Es Pujols	4	10	5	14	8	9	-	10	14	5	9	3	2	5	16
Es Arenals	10	16	9	20	2	15	10	-	6	14	15	10	8	11	8
La Mola	14	20	13	24	6	19	14	6	-	18	19	14	12	15	2
La Savina	8	8	9	12	12	7	5	14	18	-	3	8	6	3	20
Porto Sale	9	9	10	13	13	8	9	15	19	3	-	9	7	4	21
Punta Prima	4	10	5	14	8	9	3	10	14	8	9	-	2	5	16
Sant Ferran	2	8	3	12	6	7	2	8	12	6	7	2	-	3	14
Sant Francesc	5	5	6	9	9	4	5	11	15	3	4	5	3	-	17
Es Far de la Mola	16	22	15	26	8	21	16	8	2	20	21	16	14	17	-

Formentera Map (for detailed maps see back of book)

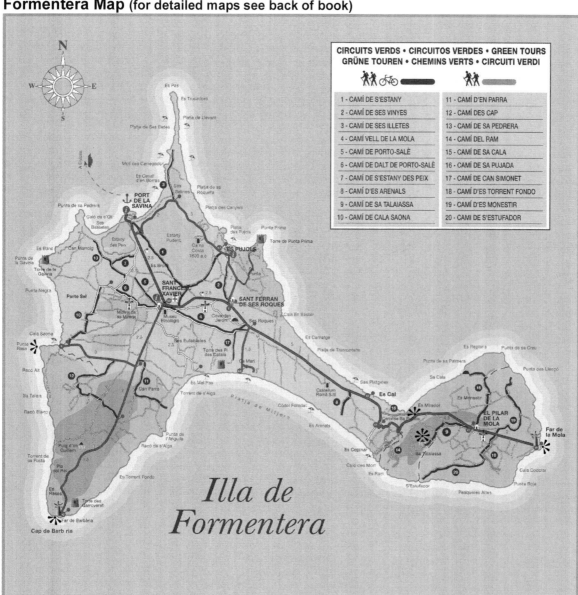

In the map above, provided by the local tourist office, the main roads are marked in red, and the hiking and biking trails are marked in blue. The PM-820 cuts across the island from north-west to south-east. The road extending south out of Sant Francesc is the PM-820-1, and the road that runs from Sant Ferran along the northern side of the inland salt lake Estany Pudent is the PM-820-2.

The contrasts of the island's geography, from its narrow northern peninsula to the steep cliffs of la Mola, can only be fully appreciated by making the trip and seeing them for yourself.

1.2. Weather

The climate on Formentera is sub arid, and the long hot summers can hit the mid-80s in August. The heat is amplified when the dry *leveche* wind blows across from Africa, but most of the time the local wind has a cooling effect.

From May to September the island enjoys over 10 hours of sunshine every day, and this halves during the winter months. The winters are fairly mild, with temperatures of around 60 degrees Fahrenheit between November and April.

The off-season weather is not harsh at all: I spent a very enjoyable November and December on the island and was able to swim and sunbathe on all but a handful of the days (mind you the sea was a bit chilly in December, so swimming is not for everyone). The coldest the sea drops to is 55 degrees Fahrenheit in February. In August it spikes at around 77 Fahrenheit, but in the shallow waters it feels a lot warmer.

March and October are the wettest months with two to three inches of rain, but outside these months rainfall is limited.

1.3.   History

Formentera has a number of prehistoric sites evidencing that the island was inhabited as long ago as 4,000 years. The Phoenicians, Carthaginians and the Romans were all attracted to the island despite its lack of a natural water supply.

Megalithic Remains in Cap de Barbaria

The Roman Road

One of the first references in literature comes from the Greek geographer Strabo (63BC-24AD) who named the island Ophiusa, which means land of snakes. This could be an indication that the indigenous lizards have always been plentiful, or maybe the island was named this way to ward off unwelcome visitors.

The Romans farmed it, and gave it the name Frumentaria, meaning Island of Wheat, although their main export was actually dried figs. They built a port in Es Calo, and behind it at Castell Roma de Can Blai is a camp that was used to watch over the harbour.

After the Romans came the Vandals, followed by Byzantines, Arabs, Normans, and finally the Catalans. It was in 1235 that the island was conquered by the Catalan-Aragonese crown, and the majority of the Muslim population was exterminated. The Catalans set up four administrative sections, but they couldn't maintain an organized island in the face of persistent pirate attacks and illness. Thus in the 14th Century Formentera was abandoned and became a base for the Barbary and Turkish pirates.

In 1697 Carlos II of Spain decided to resettle the island. Under Carlos II's instruction sea captain Marc Ferrer came, and built the defence towers to keep the pirates at bay. It was in 1889 that Formentera formed an independent municipality with Ibiza, "Consell Insular d'Eivissa i Formentera" and in 2007 Formentera formed an independent municipality, "Consell Insular de Formentera."

The manufacture of salt and the farming of dry fruit trees, such as figs, olives and almonds, were the island's main industries up until a tourism boom in the 1950s. The unspoiled nature of the island attracted a wave of hippies, and the island retains the hippy culture to this day.

1.4.   Formentera in Popular Culture

Formentera has made a few appearances in literature since the Greek geographer Strabo mentioned it over 2,000 years ago. For example, the lighthouse Far de la Mola inspired Jules Verne to write 'Off on a Comet' back in 1877 and there is a monument noting this at the lighthouse. More recently one of the island's caves, Sa Cova Foradada, was featured in the film 'Lucia y el Sexo.'

2. Villages

2.1.   La Savina

With no airport most visitors arrive at Formentera via its port of La Savina. It is a natural harbour that was used for the export of salt and planks of Sabina pine. The port was separated from the mainland until the 1930s when a breakwater was constructed.

It has a modern marina, and there is some serious money calling at port alongside the neo-hippies that take the ferries. La Savina rivals Monaco from the value of boats per cubic meter during the summer months.

Throughout the year there are multiple daily ferries between Ibiza and Formentera, and during the summer season there are also boats from Sant Antoni, Santa Eularia, Palma, Barcelona, Altea, Alicante and Denia (there aren't direct boats from Palma, Barcelona, Altea or Alicante – they are always via Ibiza). La Savina is also the departure point for day trips to Espalmador.

A Modern Marina

Balearia Ferry

From what used to be nothing more than a fisherman's wharf, it has expanded into a pretty decent harbour. Most of the shops are dedicated to serving tourists fresh of the ferry, with a wealth of rental bikes, rental car and water sport shops. The restaurants overlooking the marina serve great tapas, although funnily enough not the best fish – for this you should head to the restaurants of Es Calo. If you are arriving for the day then you should call in at the tourist office and get a map. The staff there is very friendly and will help you plan an itinerary to meet your needs.

Port de la Savina also backs on to Estany des Peix and the salt pans of Ses Salines. These are rich in natural beauty, and if you happen to be an ornithologist then you will be more than satisfied keeping an eye out for the 210 species that have been sighted. You are also within a 30 minute walk of the beaches of Es Trucadors.

Opposite the north western point of Estany Pudent, Sa Sequia, you will see that there are large holes carved out of the rock next to the sea – these crude basins were used for fish farming. Past Sa Sequia you will see an old triangular building, where bombs and gas were stored for planes during the Second World War.

2.2.   Sant Francesc Xavier

With a population in the thousands Sant Francesc is one of the quietest capitals in Europe. Just over a mile (2km) south-east from La Savina its main attraction is the square known as Plaça de la Constitució. Despite being the capital it is not really the social centre of the village, and the bars don't even stay open past midnight.

The square does not have much more than a couple of benches around some olive trees, and the Church Esglesia de Sant Francesc Xavier. The church was built between 1726 and 1738, and its fortress-like façade is by design as the church was used as a refuge from the Barbary pirates and even had cannons installed on its roof. It was mainly women who hid in the church as the pirates often chose to strike when the men were following the red tuna route to the tuna's breeding ground in the Gulf of Mexico.

Church Esglesia de Sant Francesc Xavier

If you look carefully at the church façade you will see that it does have one small window. As you step inside you should take a look at the baptismal font, which was built 1,000 years before the main church. The faded sculptures behind it are eerie rather than beautiful. It is thought to come from an old monastery in la Mola, and possibly dates back to the Germanic Vandals. Walking on into the church you will note that it has a narrow nave, a gold plated alter, and five small side chapels.

Connected to the Church is the old government building, and opposite it is the new one – the Casa de sa Constitucio. The cistern that is just to the right of the church was one of the first public services on the island.

The current church was preceded by Capella de sa Tanca, or Tanca Vella, which is a 14th century building. For further details see Section 4.

Sant Francesc Second Hand Market

2.3.   Sant Ferran de ses Roques

Sant Ferran is the most centrally located of Formentera's villages and has a lot going for it as a base from which to explore the island. However, it has not always been in its current location, as it was previously nearer to the saltwater lagoon of Estany Pudent.

It was named in memory of King Ferdinand the Catholic and its full name is Sant Ferran de ses Roques in Catalan, or San Fernando in Spanish. With two flour mills and a church dating back to the eighteenth century it is clear that it has long been a focal point of the island. It has continued to grow, and the resulting architecture is not always pretty. As you come from Es Pujols the apartment blocks look distinctly drab, but on the plus side the village is very functional with banks, a post office, internet café, and an excellent doctor's surgery.

Esglesia de Sant Ferran

Sant Ferran Bar

If you leave the main streets and head up the cobbled path to the Esglesia de Sant Ferran you reach a prettier area. There used to be a church located closer to the salt pans, but a new church was established when the rest of the village moved in 1883 because the saltpan ground was not firm enough and village buildings started to crumble. The fact that the sandstone facade has not been whitewashed distinguishes it from most Balearic churches.

Opposite the church is La Fonda Pepe, which is still living off its reputation as a hippy hang out (Dylan spent a lot of time here), and when you observe the clientele you will note that someone forgot to tell a few of the residents that the 1960s are over. Formentera has a stronger trace of the hippy movement than Ibiza and Fonda Pepe is the perfect place to soak it up. You can also visit the local guitar workshop which has been handcrafting instruments for rock stars and holidaymakers alike for decades. The most famous customers are Pink Floyd, who no doubt hung out at Fonda Pepe whilst waiting for their bespoke guitars.

If you decide to make Sant Ferran your base then there are vineyards and farmland around the village that offer a good range of accommodation, in far more attractive surroundings than the centre. If you head up towards the countryside next to Esglesia de Sant Ferran you will see that this area known as Venda de ses Roques has plenty of traditional farmhouses. The alternative is the vineyard on the other side of the village. These are a great spot because you are just five minutes away from the action of Es Pujols without being exposed to its throng of young holidaymakers 24 hours a day.

In terms of sites Cova d'en Xeroni is just down the road. A local farmer found these caves when he was digging a well, and many a disappointed tourist wishes that he hadn't. The stalactites and stalagmites are nothing special really. To get there you head just past the 6km point of the PM-820 and turn right opposite the Spar supermarket.

Cova d'en Xeroni

13/97

2.4. El Pilar de la Mola

Although it is just 11 kilometres from Sant Ferran, El Pilar feels very distinct from the rest of the island. Perhaps it is the steep incline that you need to overcome to get there that contributes to this sense of divide, maybe it is the dark passage of pine trees that you go through to enter the village that makes it feel other-worldly, or it could just be the location at the edge of the island. Whatever, the reasons, it is true to say that the El Pilar population don't leave their part of the town too often, and have developed a locals mentality within an island of just 9,500 people. And this is no bad thing. You really do get the sense of coming to a different place. There are some on Formentera who use the terms 'molers' for the residents of this area and 'baixers' for the rest of the population, with baixer meaning 'from below.'

The cycle up to El Pilar is pretty tough, but it can be done in less than an hour from Es Calo, and that includes some time for walking up the steeper inclines, and pausing at the bus stop on the right to admire the panoramic views looking out across the Es Carnatge isthmus and over to Ibiza. Just next to the bus stop is the El Mirador restaurant, but if you want to enjoy the views from a seated position, with a cool drink in your hand, then make sure you book in advance as it gets extremely busy in the summer.

La Mola Countryside

If you enter El Pilar on a bicycle and keep peddling, then you will exit the village in two minutes – it is small! It is just a strip with a few restaurants and farmhouses, with acres of farmland behind it. There are around 50 houses in the village and it is mainly farmers who live here.

Taberna Can Blaiet La Mola is the first restaurant as you come into town on the left, and it also doubles up as the village post office. The church Esglesia del Pilar de la Mola was built between 1772 and 1784 in the typical whitewashed style of Ibiza, and is fairly unremarkable.

The windmill of Moli Vell is just outside the village and although it was built in 1778 still works. Rumour has it that Bob Dylan lived inside Moli Vell in the 1960s. I wonder how he got to La Fonda Pepe every day?

The highest point of the island at 663 feet (202m) is Sa Talaiassa. This is located south-west of the village, and is on Route No.9 of the Circuits Verds (green path cycling route). If you make it up to Sa Talaiasaa then to the east you will see fields of farmland with figs, wheat and vines, which were first tended to by the Augustinian monks of the thirteenth century. The dry stone boundary walls (parets seques) that are typical of Balearic farmland mark out the farms. As you get closer to the sea there are some spectacular cliff top views, with the limestone cliffs over 190 meters in height at some points.

Biking Trails around La Mola

La Mola Countryside

If you stay in El Pilar for an extended period then it is one of the few places on Formentera where you need some form of motorized transport. Even if you are just planning to chill out in Es Calo, then cycling the hill on a daily basis is probably not on the agenda of most holidaymakers.

La Mola Craft Fair

The La Mola craft fair has been running since 1984. It starts up in early May, and runs every Wednesday and Sunday until the 12th October. Many of the people at the fair make their living from selling the arts and crafts on display. In addition to the arts and crafts there are entertainers such as musicians and jugglers making it an enjoyable day out. It's a good place to get a souvenir and have some fun.

Sellers are issued with a craft guarantee certificate which is issued by the Formentera Municipal Council and the Formentera Association of Craftspeople to show that the products have been designed and made in local workshops, and if you are interested many of the workshops are available to visit.

Some of the gifts to consider are the local grass sandals known as *espardenyes*, and there is also a lot of local food produce, including wine, figs and cheese.

2.5.   Far de la Mola

From El Pilar de la Mola you see the lighthouse of Far de la Mola in the distance. It's a two and a half kilometre strip through stark farmlands to get there, and you are rewarded with stunning cliff top views looking out to Cala Codolar in the south and Punta des Lençol in the north. Standing in the desert like terrain of El Pilar de la Mola, with the Mediterranean Sea stretching as far as the eye can see, you really do feel like you are at the edge of the earth. Most other parts of the island have views to Ibiza or other Formentera beaches, but here it is just you and the lizards. If you are lucky you will see some of the peregrine falcons that nest in the cliffs, and failing that you should at least see some of the rock sparrows that enjoy the barren terrain.

Far de la Mola Lighthouse

La Mola Cliffs

The lighthouse was the only one on the island until the lighthouse of Far de Barbaria was built. It was built during the reign of Isabel II in 1861 and there is a monument noting that it inspired Jules Verne to write 'Off on a Comet' back in 1877. The tower is over 20 meters in height and is an important guide for ships passing to the south of the islands; it has a listed range of 23 nautical miles (42.5 km, 26.5 mi). Up until the mid-twentieth century the fuel needed to power it was delivered via the cove of Es Codolar, which is just south of the lighthouse.

You can just about see Mallorca on a clear day.

Trip Suggestion
You can head south on Route No.20, which is Cami de s'Estufador. It's a steep decline that takes you through the charcoal stacks (estufas) that gives the S'Estufador coastline its name.

3. Beaches

The unusual geological evolution of the island has created a variety of beaches. The central, narrow part of the island known as Es Carnatge has the rocky Tramuntana coastline on its north face, and the sandy Platja de Mitjorn on the south. The northern peninsula has back to back beaches with no buildings in sight, and there are also various bays, such as the natural cove of Cala Saona. Formentera's beaches have a number of natural advantages: with no plankton in the waters they remain crystal clear, and the island's shape protects the southern beaches when the winds are up on the northern beaches.

In total Formentera has over 20 kilometres of beaches, from rocky coves through to white sand beaches stretching out along the sea for kilometres. What you will notice about most of the beaches is the almost total absence of buildings, and those that do have construction have significant height restrictions. The Blue Flag Programme, owned and run by the independent non-profit organisation Foundation for Environmental Education, has awarded its mark to many of the island's pristine beaches.

In this section let's take a look at some of the more popular beaches.

Ses Arenals

3.1. Es Cavall d'en Borras and Moli des Carregador

Running up from Port de la Savina is the coast of Es Cavall d'en Borras, which is made up of two sections known as Cala Savina and Es Carregador. Really it is little more than a strip of land that keeps Estany Pudent out of the sea. There is some protection from the Sabina trees, but it can get pretty blustery. The old mill, Moli des Carregador, marks the end of this strip of coastline.

Es Cavall d'en Borras

Path to Es Trucadors

3.2.   Es Trucadors

The Trucador peninsula is a long stretch of flat land, reaching out from the north of Formentera that almost connects to the neighbouring island of Espalmador. It is made up of seemingly endless white beaches, and shallow turquoise waters. These beaches, along with Es Pujols, are some of the busiest as they attract a lot of day trippers from Ibiza, and you will see quite a few boats anchored off the coast in the summer.

To get there you head up the coastline that stretches out from Port de la Savina. You can cycle or walk from La Savina, and there is a path that takes you up the rugged and rocky strip of Es Cavall d'en Borras. You will pass over the inlet that lets in fresh seawater to Ses Salines and Estany Pudent to keep them from smelling too bad in the summer, and then continue through pines and dunes, until you reach Moli des Carregador. Formerly a mill to pump seawater into the salt pans it is now a restaurant with better views than food.

The inlet into Estant Pudent

Platja de Llevant

Past Moli des Carregador the peninsula has Platja de Ses Illetes running along its western edge, and Platja de Levant on the east. Ses Illetes is a chain of coves that look out onto the five islets from which it gets its name. The main islets are Illa Tramuntana, Illa Rodona, and Illa des Pouet. As you walk northbound you can drop in on each of the coves that make up Ses Illetes: Big Sur, El Tiburon, Es Moli de Sal, El Pirata, Juan y Andrea and Es Ministere.

Platja de Levant is a straight strip of land made up of Llevant Beach. It is an incredible stretch of totally undeveloped coastline. The waters here are still and shallow, and it is one of the few high quality European beaches that doesn't have a resort hotel built on top of it. As you continue south you reach Ses Salines, Platja de Sa Roqueta and Platja des Canyes.

At the northern tip of Es Trucadors is Es Pas, which is a sand strip connecting to Espalmador. But the strip is just below the sea, and some potentially strong currents, so you should not attempt the crossing. But it is well worth heading up there as just before Es Pas is a 30 meter strip of sand with the sea on either side. Most people agree that these are the island's best beaches. Staying until early evening to watch the sun set behind Es Vedra is an experience worth waiting for.

Path to El Tiburon

Beach at Es Ministere

The breezes only affect one side of Es Trucadors at a time, and you are never more than a two minute walk from one side to the other so you can have a wind free day without too much bother. Although there is a lack of restaurants, the chiringuitos sell snacks. You can rent all the equipment you need for water sports here.

3.3.   Illa de S'Espalmador

Espalmador is a private island just north of Formentera. Despite being owned by a wealthy Barcelona family anyone can visit its white beaches, natural coves, and sulphurous mud baths. It is an unspoiled paradise, and other than the remains of an old defence tower that was used to spot Barbary pirates, there are no buildings on the island.

Getting There

The recommend way to get there is via the regular boat trips from the port of La Savina, or the beach of Ses Illetes. Some guide books suggest you can walk across the shallow waters that lap between Formentera and Espalmador, but this is extremely irresponsible advice. The stretch of water is known as Pas d´en Adolf, or Es Pas de s´Espalmador.

On a day when the waters are completely still and there is not a breeze in the air, then yes it is technically possible to walk across, but with even the slightest winds then it is a perilous journey. There have been fatalities, with tourists falling victim to the strong current. When taking the ferry between Ibiza and Formentera you can feel this passage of water (Es Freus) dragging the boat off its course, and it is this same current that runs between Espalmador and Formentera. So please do not walk across no matter what others may be doing or saying. A healthy respect for the sea will keep you safe.

The ferries to Espalmador leave from La Savina, and stop at the beach of Illetes before dropping anchor. Generally departures run from 10:15 to 11:45, with a final ferry at 13:15. Returns go from 16:15 to 17:30, with a final ferry at 18:45. These excursions cost 15 euros, but you should check the times and pricing on arrival. There are also a number of daily charters from Ibiza, and from the beach you will see a mass of beautiful yachts. If you have some binoculars trained on Marc Jacobs' boat you may even catch sightings of Kate Moss.

View of Espalmador

Route to Es Pas de s´Espalmador

Mud Baths

One of the delights of Espalmador is mud bathing. Right in the middle of this tranquil island is a natural mud bath that's easy to find. Head along the far north end of Platja de s'Alga (s'Alga beach) and follow the narrow pathway through the scrubland that backs the beach. Finally you will emerge at a wide salt plain that has liquid mud at its centre. In years with light rainfall the sulphurous mud pond is dry across much of its four hectares.

Although it has no proven therapeutic benefits, on a hot sunny day there's nothing nicer than rolling about or wallowing in cooling mud. Let it dry as you walk back to the beach then dive into the clear sea to get clean. A common sight is naturists emerging clothed in black mud, only to then wash it off in the sea and appear naked once more.

Unfortunately not all people treat the mud baths with respect – they throw mud at one another and the surrounding area. In the summer of 2009 this led to such significant damage that the baths were shut. With Espalmador a private island it is important to remember that access to it is a privilege, and the baths should be bathed in, not played in. Note: at the time of writing the mud paths are used for nesting birds and it is forbidden to use them.

Beaches
The best beach on Espalmador is Platja de S'Alga and it is here that you will find the highest concentration of naturists, although nudism is not obligatory. It has shallow warm waters and pristine white beaches that bring hoards of day trippers from Ibiza who never make it as far as Formentera. Also worth a look are the coves of Cala de Bocs and the sa Torreta beach in the north-west.

Defence Tower
Espalmador has a defence tower Torre de S'Espalmador and you can see it by heading over to Sa Guadiola. Also known as the tower of Guardiola, it has been restored and having been built between 1749 and 1750 is older than four defence towers on Formentera.

Other Islands
Besides Espalmador there are a number of other outlying islands, one of which is Illa d'es Penjats – the Island of the Hanged. It takes its name from the fact that pirates were executed here as far back as 1271. Illes Negres, the Black Islands, lie to the west of Penjats, and Illa des Porcs (Pig Island) and Illas des Torretes (Turret Island) are two others. Pig Island is notable for its lighthouse, but Turret Island is absent of the defensive structures you might expect given its name. Espardell used to be home to goats, but now has rabbits, lizards and cormorants.

3.4.   Platja de ses Canyes
This beach is a small strip 85 meters long and an average of 12 meters deep. It has calm waters and is located just outside Es Pujols on the road to Es Trucadors. The beach is surrounded by steep cliffs, and you have to go up a small incline to reach it.

Route to Platja de ses Canyes

Platja de ses Canyes

3.5. Ses Salines

The beach that runs behind salts works, just down from Platja de Llevant shares the same name as the salt pans. It is protected by a long dune, and is just two kilometres from Es Pujols. The water here can get a bit choppy, even in the summer.

3.6. Cala Saona

If you take the main road west from Sant Francesc and then after 2.5 kilometres take the road running south-west you will travel through fields of carob and fig, and Aleppo pine. Three kilometres later you get to the cove of Cala Saona. The cove is low lying as a result of a structural fault, and differential erosion has created a beach of just 140 meters across, but 120 meters in depth.

In its day Cala Saona had 400 ships anchored at port, but when you lie on the beach it's difficult to imagine the hustle and bustle of the sixteenth century. These days there are just a few of the wooden *escars* used to shelter small fishing boats. It was also used as a place to breed and train falcons, but spotting a bird of prey in this location is unlikely these days.

Cala Saona Beach

Views from Cala Saona Beach

What makes Cala Saona such a great location is the surrounding farmland and cliff top walks that you can take. The views looking down from the peak of Punta Rasa make it worth the 30 minute hike: you will see some deep yet crystal clear waters battering the cliffs, and on a good day can see as far as Denia. The waters around Punta Rasa are popular with divers as there are plenty of caves to explore.

The Hotel Cala Saona is right on the beach if you want to make this area your base. The building is ugly, but the views from your room are anything but.

3.7.　Tramuntana

The erosion that has taken place in Tramuntana makes for an interesting landscape. It runs for around five kilometres up to Ses Plagetes. If you are seeking some privacy then exploring Tramuntana will pay dividends as there are a few sandy beaches lurking through the rocks waiting for those that take the time to find them.

Tramuntana Rock Pool

Views from Tramuntana

3.8.　Platja de Mitjorn

Running across Formentera's south coast is Platja de Mitjorn, which at five kilometres in length is the longest beach on the island. Platja de Mitjorn means 'midday beach' and it has areas of rocky coastline interspersed with sandy beaches, running from Es Pal Mas to Es Copinar. The section between Ca Mari and Ses Arenals is the most popular, and nudist bathing is common. The main developments on the beach are at either end, and for the most part it is a strip of unspoiled coastline that gives Es Trucadors a run for its money.

Platja de Mitjorn

Pathway behind Mitjorn

When you are travelling along the PM820 you will see multiple roads leading to the different areas that make up Platja de Mitjorn. If you are heading east out of Sant Ferran then the first beach that you will see to your right is Ca Mari. The defence tower of Es Pi d'es Catala is located on the western part of the beach, and it is a great vantage point from which to view all the areas that make up Mitjorn: Es Ca Mari, Raco Fondo, Es Codol Foradat, Els Valencians, Es Alrenals and Maryland.

To get to the most beautiful part of the beach you should turn at the 8km point of the PM-820. Lucky and Blue Bar are two local institutions that have based themselves here. Lucky is an Italian restaurant with a relaxed ambiance. It is not too expensive and usually has good fresh fish. After a lunch at Lucky you can head to Blue Bar which has a terrace overlooking the sea. Most people come for the ambient music and hippy-appeal, but the restaurant is pretty decent too.

Further east are the Maryland (Es Copinar) and ses Arenals beaches. To access the area you can take the PM-820 and turn off at the 13km mark when you see the large sign for the Riu hotel. This area has more of a resort feel to it, but is still quieter than Es Pujols. If you would prefer one of the more traditional spots, then El Torrent de s'Alga is still used by the local fishermen as a harbour.

Ses Arenals

Las Banderas

If you decide to stay near Mitjorn then I recommend the area around Es Ca Mari, as it has a range of pretty accommodation up a short hill. It's a good location because you are also close to the Spar supermarket and Sant Ferran. You will have a more authentic holiday at one of the pensions or farmhouses in this area than you would at one of the large hotels.

3.9. Es Calo & Ses Platgetes

Before the La Savina port was developed, Es Calo was the island's main harbour. Although just 100 feet (30m) across it was selected by the Romans to export figs, and later as a place for the residents of La Mola to drop anchor. In fact, the village gets its name of Es Calo de Sant Agusti from the fact that the monks from La Mola used to moor their boats here, before heading up Cami Roma (de sa Pujada) to their monastery. Right up until the 1920s it was used for shipping sandstone, charcoal and wood. Today you will see that is still used by a number of fishing boats, and as an old fisherman's town it has the best fish restaurants in town: Pascual and Can Rafalet.

Since the northern coast is windier and rockier than that on the south, tourists often start their day here, and then cross the road to Mitjorn if the winds get up. The rocks beneath the water are home to some interesting marine life so you should get your snorkel out before heading up to the white sands of Ses Platgetes.

Ses Platgetes is just five minutes away from Es Calo and in addition to its white beaches has some decent dunes protecting you from winds, and great views of the La Mola cliffs.

Ses Platgetes

Day Trip Suggestion
Go to Es Calo, enjoy Ses Platgetes and a coffee at the harbour before walking via Cami Roma to the El Mirador restaurant. Take in its views across the isthmus while you have lunch, and then back track to Es Calo.

3.10. Es Pujols

The Es Pujols beach is made up of two white sand crescents and turquoise waters that are so shallow they reach tropical temperatures during the summer. You can also enjoy swimming out to the small islets that peek out of the water.

Even though Es Pujols is the island's only resort area it still retains some character with ramshackle fishing huts at either end of the beach. There is a ramp for disabled access into the water, and the company Wet4Fun provides all the rental gear you need for any water sports.

Avenida Miramar is the promenade overlooking the beach, and behind that is a network of streets with boutiques, cafes and restaurants. The main High Street of Passeig des Palmeres

also has plenty of shopping streets. In the evening there is a bustling trade at the market stalls which line the streets.

Es Pujols Beach

Es Pujols Hotel

Es Pujols has the island's highest concentration of accommodation, and the island's most lively nightlife is here. However, even though this is the place to go for young Germans and Italians it is nothing like as wild as Ibiza. Xueno is one of the more popular clubs.

4. Places of Interest

4.1.   Estany Pudent

Estany Pudent is the largest of Formentera's two salt lagoons. It starts south of the Port de la Savina, and is just behind the coastline of Es Cavall d'en Borras (although it takes in fresh seawater from Sa Sequi).

The history (some say legend) behind Estany Pudent is an interesting one. In the 1800s two sisters came from Ibiza to raise animals on Formentera's land, and after a long drought one of them ran out of water. Even though the other sister had the large Can Marroig well on her land she would not share its water and sent her sibling packing. However, following the drought came a flood, and the selfish sister's land was flooded to the extent that it became what is known today as Estany Pudent. On a clear day you can see the remains of a finca under the water.

You can cycle around this inland lake via the Circuits Verds, or Green Tours, which are the designated cycling and hiking paths of the island.

It is Route No.1 that loops around Estany Pudent. There are a number of access points to the route:

- As you exit La Savina you can turn left after 500m towards the salt pans, and you will see a dirt track on your right.
- If you are coming from Sant Francesc you can access the path by taking the road to the hospital, but instead of turning into the hospital carry straight on.
- If you are coming from Es Pujols take the road to Platja de sa Roqueta and turn left before the Argentine restaurant.

Estany Pudent Wetlands

Estany Pudent can be translated as 'stinky pond' or 'stagnant pond,' and on a hot summer day the combination of sulphur fumes and decomposing algae can whip up quite a stench. Not to mention that the accumulated rainwater makes it an ideal breeding ground for swarms of mosquitoes. Despite these negatives it is an area worth exploring.

Although the salt concentration is up to three times higher than that in the sea, Estany Pudent sustains many beautiful freshwater plants, and the surrounding wetlands are rich in wildlife. Most of the plant life is the salt tolerant salcornia species, more commonly known as glasswort or pickleweed. The birds that you might spot include: the spotted redshank, great reed warblers

and the black-winged stilt. In fact this place used to known as the Flamingo Lagoon because of the large numbers of flamingos, but these days it is more of a rarity to spot one of these. The black-crested grebe spends its winters here, and other birds include the Kentish plover, spotted redshanks, herons and egrets.

The lake is right next to Ses Salines – the salt beds. These are the site of the traditional salt manufacture which used to support the islands. These days they are just there for display really, although occasionally one of the older generation might step out and do a bit of salt harvesting for old times' sake. Along the north-west of the lagoon is where the old salt train used to take the salt down to the port of La Savina. These days you can still see the train behind the Museum of Ethnography.

You probably wouldn't fancy swimming in Estany Pudent, but just in case you do please note that it is prohibited. With so many beautiful beaches it's no loss.

4.2.   Estany des Peix

The smaller of Formentera's two salt water lagoons, Estany des Peix is particularly popular with the French for some reason. It is located just one kilometre south of La Savina and is on the right and side as you take the PM-820 out of the village.

Estany des Peix used to be an old fishing port, thus the name Peix and connects to the sea via a narrow mouth, named Sa Boca. The width of Sa Boca means that only the smallest boats drop anchor here.

The calm, shallow waters make it ideal for water sports, and it is a great place to try out kayaking, windsurfing or sailing. The waters also have more to offer than just water sports: Yondelis is a new anti-tumour drug derived from the marine organism, Ecteinascidia turbinata, a 'sea squirt', or tunicate, found in the lagoon.

Estany des Peix

Small Boats Only at des Peix

The track around the lagoon is ideal for nature lovers, and there is a path that leads to Can Marroig. There are a number of marsh plants growing, mainly from the salicornia genus, and in amongst the rushes and glasswort plants are a wide variety of birds. With the proximity to the sea you are likely to spot seabirds such as gulls, and there are also plenty of terns, ducks and waders.

4.3.   Can Marroig

Can Marroig is a public farm in the north easy of Formentera covering 137.33 hectares, which was acquired by the autonomous region in 1998. Parts of the property date back to 1620, and the main house and farmyard is constructed in a typical Mallorcan style. Technically the Can Marroig area includes Torre de Punta Gavina.

The house at Can Marroig was formerly La Hotel Anglais and has a history that is of particular interest to Europe's Jewish population. Whilst Mallorca was the scene of terrible anti-Jewish outrages following the Spanish Inquisition in the fifteenth century, the Jewish community in Formentera lived quietly, yet peacefully. After the establishment of the Inquisition in 1410, the Vicars General of the Inquisition who came to Formentera on inspection tours left satisfied that "no one practiced the Laws of Moses or Mohomet."

However, by the time of the 1930s the Jewish population was once again under threat, and Can Marroig was opened as a pension at that time. This was a cover to allay suspicions about the number of visitors that it started getting. It is now known that these visitors were visiting a secret synagogue in the cellar.

4.4.   Ses Salines

The Ses Salines Natural Park covers a wide area, including the Es Trucadors peninsula and its surrounding sea. It extends to the wetlands that run around Estany Pudent and Estany des Peix, and it is also the term used to describe the old salt pans.

The salt works themselves closed down in 1984, but they remain part of the conservation area. Even though the salt pans are no longer used commercially the process of salt crystallization still continues and you see froth washing up against the walls of the salt pans, and on windy days it blows across the roads. The salt pans work by letting in water from Estany Pudent, which has a higher concentration of salt than the sea, and from there it crystallizes, with sluice gates opened to help water evaporate.

Around Ses Salines

The mill wheel that was used to pump the salt pans was build in the UK town of Accrington. Unfortunately it was ordered in meters, but was built in feet and inches so the wheel house had to be rebuilt once the wheel arrived. The wheel is on the right as you go into Es Pujols from La Savina.

The area attracts wading birds that like living in mud, so-called limicolous birds. Although the wetlands are teeming with wildlife, the adventurous ornithologist can move off land into Es Freus to look for storm petrel, the Balearic shearwater, fisher eagles, cormorants, yellow-legged gull, and Audouin's gull. Below the surface are the sea grass plants known as posidonia. The channel between Formentera and Ibiza is home to the longest living matter ever discovered: a posidonia plant eight miles long.

178 plant species have been identified in Ses Salines, including salicornia and halophilic vegetation.

4.5. Punta Pedrera

Just northwest of Estany des Peix is Punta de Sa Pedrera. This is worth visiting for its unusual rock formation. This was where sandstone used to be excavated for export, and in Roman times was used as a port. It is the excavation that has created the unusual formation which looks like an array of swimming pools. The best way to see this part of the island is on a boat, as you will also be able to see some half-submerged caves.

4.6.   Defence Towers

Formentera has four defence towers, built on strategic points of the island's coastline during the eighteenth century. There is also a fifth tower on Espalmador. Formentera has been an important location since the oriental shipping route, the Strait of Ses Portes, was used by ships that came from the East from 1000 BC to get metals from the Kingdom of Tartessos. This strategic location made the island a target for invasion, and it was deserted in the fourteenth century after people became so fed up with being attacked. Barbary pirates made use of it as a place of rest for the next few centuries, and it wasn't until there was a let up in piracy that the island repopulated in the eighteenth century, and the defence towers were built.

The Defence Towers
-    Torre des Pi des Catala
-    Torre de Punta Prima
-    Torre de la Gavina
-    Torre des Garroveret
-    Torre de S'Espalmador

The sixth defence tower might be said to be the Church in Saint Francesc, which at the time it was built could have housed the entire population. There were two cannons on the roof, and Formentera acted as an early warning system to Ibiza by lighting fires and sending smoke signals from the roof of the church.

4.6.1. Torre des Pi des Catala

The quickest route to Torre des Pi des Catala is to turn off Route 4: if you are coming from the Eastern/Sant Ferran end of Route 4 then you would turn off left a few hundred meters after the entrance to Route 17.

Just after this gorgeous farmhouse…   **turn into this road.**

You then ride through a country lane, and you will see the tower on your left just before you reach the coastline. The three times that I took this route I met a very large dog that has a vociferous bark, but not bite – if you see him just pedal fast! To access the tower itself you climb up through the dunes from the coast.

However, the quickest route is not the best. If you take green route 17 to the Mitjorn beach and turn right, you can then cycle along the coastline until you hit a small road, and if you look up to your right at that point you will see the defence tower. The tower itself is one of the few that you can walk inside, but unfortunately this has given rise to vandalism, and defacement of the property. Unless, Osama really did hide there!

Torre des Pi des Catala

From the tower you get an excellent view of all the parts of Platja de Mitjorn, and of the Mola plateau.

The site saw some action in 1813 when Torre des Pi des Catala was used to fire at a French boat of 40 sailors who fled under the attack. Little did they know that there were just six men firing upon them from the tower.

4.6.2. Torre de Punta Prima

Getting up to this Tower is a leisurely cycle from Es Pujols, and is worth it for the cliff top views. The standard route is to take the road just opposite the supermarket in between Es Pujols and Sant Ferran. On your way back from the tower you may want to branch off to the dirt tracks on the right. One of these connects to the eastern end of the Es Pujols beach and is a nice shortcut.

Torre de Punta Prima

Punta Prima Views

4.6.3. Torre de la Gavina

This is the least accessible of the defence towers, but is worth the effort because of the views out to Es Vedra. To get to the defence tower you can take Green Route No.6 from Sant Francesc, and when you reach the bending road which marks the end of the route just follow it as it bears left away from Estany des Peix. This will take you to the entrance of Route No.10, an unmarked dirt path, to the right of which you will see the road sign below.

This sign reads, 'Cami de Dalt de Porto Sale'

You want to take this road, which is so bumpy there are quite a few occasions on which you will want to dismount from your bike to avoid punctures (not to mention haemorrhoids). You just keep going straight until you come across a sign for a no-through road, and you take that road! Eventually you will come to a low wall, and if you look over you will see a dirt track continues on the other side, so just hop on over and continue to Punta de la Gavina. After a few hundred meters you will want to park your bike as the size of the rocks increase, and you will take in some spectacular sea views across to Espalmador on one side and Punta Rasa on the other. The tower was never actually equipped with artillery, and the views are more interesting that the structure itself.

The Defence Tower and Es Vedra

Punta Rasa

This is the best place to get a view of Es Vedra and consider the many rumours and myths surrounding this small island east of Ibiza:

- That it featured in Homer
- UFO's visit the island
- Rocks were taken from Es Vedra to build the Egyptian pyramids
- The Phoenician goddess of fertility, Tanit, considered it her island
- It is the tip of Atlantis
- Ritual sacrifices to Tanit used to be performed on the island

Whether or not any of these are true you can enjoy the view. Located at Formentera's most western point the tower looked out over Es Freus, Espalmador and La Savina. Built with limestone and lime mortar this tower never had artillery and was purely a lookout point.

4.6.4. Torre de Garrovert

100 meters north east of the Far de Barbaria lighthouse is Torre de Garrovert. It looks out to the African coast, and would have been used to spot the approach of Barbary pirates.

Torre de Garrovert

Torre de Garrovert Views

4.6.5. Torre de sa Guardiola/Torre de Espalmador

This defence tower is on the Western side of Espalmador. Its name means "piggy bank tower" as it has what looks like a large money slot of its side. It is a two storey tower which was built in the eighteenth century.

4.7.   Cap de Barbaria

The name Barbaria reflects the fact that Africa's Barbary Coast is just 60 Miles (100km) away from Formentera's most southern point. But whatever the locals might tell you, I am convinced that you cannot see as far as Algeria from here. Or maybe they just eat more carrots than me.

The PMV-820-1 will take you direct from the relative hubbub of Sant Francesc to the total desolation of Cap de Barbaria. As you get closer to the lone lighthouse at the end of the road the vegetation gets ever sparser; there is a total absence of the pine trees that cover the rest of the island, and on a windy day it feels as though you could easily be blown off your bicycle. The ride is not as arduous as to Far de la Mola, as this area of elevation is not as high, and it takes less that an hour to reach Barbaria from Sant Francesc.

The reason for the lack of vegetation is deforestation during the early part of the twentieth century, and subsequent use of the land for grazing. The pine here was all used for charcoal in the 1930s, and the only plants you will see these days are rosemary and thyme.

Desolation leading to...   **a lighthouse.**

At the end of the road is a solitary lighthouse, from which you have great views of Es Vedra, Ibiza, and the second major elevation of La Mola. After checking out the lighthouse, you take a short walk up the coastline to the defence tower sat on top of some impressive cliffs.

Other Sites
As you head down from Sant Francesc there is a rest area with parking, tables, and an area for you to set up barbeque equipment. Look out for it on the right hand side around two kilometres from the light house.

South of the lighthouse is Sa Cova Foradada, which is a cave sitting 100 meters above the sea. Accessing the cave is not for the claustrophobic as you have to lower yourself through a very narrow roof.

Also, on your left as you head to the coast are a series of megalitiques – these are arrangements of stones from the megalithic era. It's no Stonehenge, but you might as well take a look. They are quite tricky to spot, so I have included the photo below so you know what to look out for (although this photo may just be enough to make you decide not to bother stopping!)

Spot the Megalithic Stones Through the Trees

Barbaria was the first area that was settled on the island, and these remains indicate that there was a large megalithic community. Archaeologists have claimed that the similarity of buildings on Formentera, and those of the Talayotic people of Mallorca and Menorca, are a sign of trade links.

Approaching Barbaria the first of the remains that you come across is the 3,800 years old Barbaria II. This Bronze Age structure is made up of a total of nine buildings, including a kiln and livestock building. Barbaria III is the remains of buildings used to keep animals, and Barbaria I is a circular group of stones which was probably a place of worship.

4.8.   Ca na Costa

The stone circle of Ca na Costa dates back to the bronze age, and its 7ft (2m) slabs make it the most significant megalithic burial ground in the Balearics. It was discovered in 1974. To get there exit Es Pujols and head north west in the direction of Platja de sa Roqueta and you will see a turning on your left clearly sign posted.

The limestone slabs, surrounded by smaller stones, are the earliest signs of people settling on the island. The stones are next to a grave which was home to eight men and two women. One of the men was over two meters in height so it is thought that he suffered from gigantism. Some speculate that he was revered for his size and thus deemed worthy of this special burial.

Ca Na Costa

The flint tools that have been found at the site are thought to come from other Balearic islands indicating that even in these early times there was a trade route. Archaeologists have dated the site to between 2,000 and 1,600 BC.

4.9.   Castellum Roma de Can Blai

Just after you pass the 10km marker when heading east on the PM-820 is a right hand turn into the remains of a Roman fort that dates back to the third century. The sandstone foundations of the perimeter wall are clear, as are the bases of five towers.

Castellum Roma

Castellum Roma is a fortress-type building that was discovered in 1979 and excavated in 1979 and 1980. It is a quadrangular structure of 40m x 40m, with five rectangular towers, two of which guard what must have been the entrance gate. It is thought that it was never actually used,

owing to the fact that neither structures nor ceramic remains have been found inside. The purpose of the fortress would have been to look out for boats coming into Es Calo, and to guard Cami Roma, which was the key road on the island at the time.

It has a similar plan to fortress constructions that defended the borders of the Empire in the Dabube, in the East, and in North Africa, which indicates that it could be dated to the Early Roman Empire. However, the exact period cannot be determined, as between the 3rd century and the Saracen invasion the Mediterranean was constantly vulnerable to attack.

4.10.   Ethnography Museum

On the main street of Sant Francesc you will find the Museu Etnologic. From an unassuming entrance next to a perfume store you climb some stairs and opposite the offices of an insurance agent is a collection of tools that were used to work the land. It's a small museum with no information in English, but it does a good job of giving a sense of what it must have been like toiling on Formentera's arid land in years gone by. It's free, so take the time to pop upstairs for 10 minutes.

One curious thing to look out for is a small train which is displayed outside in a courtyard – just exit from the back door of the second floor to take a look. The train was used to transport salt from Ses Salines to the port.

The signs inside say no photos, but the curator was kind enough to let me take a few. The collection is mainly made up of farming and fishing tools. There are also a few photos on display that show Formentera in an even less developed state.

Farming Tools

Traditional Dress

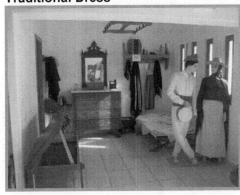

4.11.   Es Campament

Exiting La Savina on the PM-820 Es Campament is the concentration camp that was used in the years after the Spanish Civil War to hold hundreds of anti-Francoist prisoners of war. There is not much of the building remaining, but despite its views over Estany des Peix there is an uncomfortable feeling about the place. There is a plaque on display with a poem written by Joan Puig.

Remains of Es Campament

Inside Es Campament

4.12.   Sa Tanca Vella

The old church of Sa Tanca Vella is more interesting than Eglesia de Sant Francesc Xavier in many ways. Built in the 14th century it's difficult to picture a congregation squeezing into this tiny chapel. It is just over five meters in length, and two meters high.

The building was constructed from rough sandstone blocks in 1362, and then rebuilt in 1697. Until Eglesia de Sant Francesc Xavier was built in 1726 this tiny building was the island's only place of worship.

Tiny Tanca Vella

5. Green Tours Cycling & Hiking

One of the best things about Formentera is the 20 Circuits Verds, or Green Tours. These are 20 designated and signposted cycling and hiking trails that take you off the beaten path to some of the island's most beautiful spots. This section reviews every one of them.

Even if you haven't used a bike for a few years it's worth getting back in the saddle, and there is enough variety to satisfy even the seasoned cyclist. Racing bikes can head from Far de Barbaria to Far de la Mola in a few hours, and mountain bikes can explore off-road tracks, that run through nature parks, farmland, beaches, and towns.

In the Practical Guide section at the end of this book some of the rental shops are listed. They have them in every village, and there is a good stock of mountain bikes to choose from. Racing bikes are not as common so you should call in advance if you decide to rent one of those. Most stores have a policy of coming to pick you up, or do an on the spot repair, in the event that you have a puncture.

There is barely a road on the island that doesn't have cycle paths, but it is the designated Circuits Verds that you will be spending most of your time on. However, one of the frustrating things about these courses is that the starting points can be difficult to find. There is a tendency to have the entrances unmarked, and then one kilometre into the trail there is a signpost letting you know that you have indeed guessed the correct entrance. Another problem is when you reach forks in the road and there is no indication which way you should go. Although getting lost in rural Formentera can actually turn up some interesting finds, in this guide there are photos of the entrances where the signposts are missing, and tried to be as explicit as possible about how to follow the actual trails. If you take a compass with you and the relevant page then you should be fine (don't forget to print a loose leaf copy of this book before leaving for Formentera, and then you can take just the pages you need when heading out on day trips).

By linking up the villages, cycle routes and beaches you can plan some wonderful day trips on Formentera. It is always worth taking a picnic with you as there are many spots to pause and relax.

5.1. No.1: Cami d'Estany

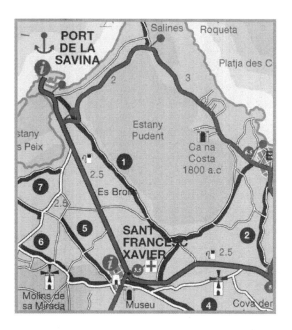

The full loop around Estany Pudent combines the road along the northern and eastern edges, with the Route No.1. The route takes you right through the wetlands, and is prime bird watching territory. Some of the birds that you might see are warblers, black-necked grebes, herons and egrets. It used to be a popular spot for flamingos, but a sighting of one is a much rarer occasion these days.

Route No.1

Home to Wildlife (and an odour)

You can access Route No.1 from three main points: a turning 500m outside la Savina, from the road that leads to the Sant Francesc Hospital, and from just outside Es Pujols. It is also accessible from a dirt track that leads down from Punta Prima.

The turning into Route No.1 after Es Pujols is just next to the Caminito restaurant.

Caminito

5.2. No.2 Cami de Ses Vinyes

When travelling between Es Pujols and Sant Ferran this is the best route by far. It is a ten minute cycle through some nice country lanes, and is named after the vineyards that line the route. The entrance ways to the path are not clearly marked, and you should look out for a small turning on the left, just fifty meters after entering Sant Ferran. Coming out of Es Pujols you will soon come across a narrow track that you turn right into.

Entrance from Sant Ferran

Entrance from Es Pujols

When you take this route from Es Pujols, you get to see just how basic the buildings of Sant Ferran are. Luckily there are some great views across farmland, out to Es Vedra on your right to distract you from the poor architecture.

5.3. No.3: Cami de Ses Illetes

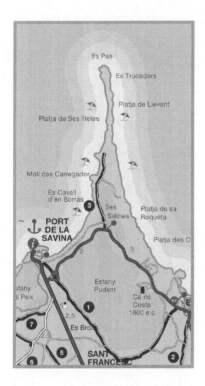

It is a rare holiday maker who visits Formentera and doesn't take a walk or cycle up Route No.3 since it leads to the most pristine white beaches on the island at Platja de Ses Illetes. The route itself is not all that attractive, as the views are mostly obscured by dunes and pines, but you can see the saltpans, and some of Es Cavall d'en Borras.

Ses Salines

5.4.   No.4: Cami Vell de la Mola

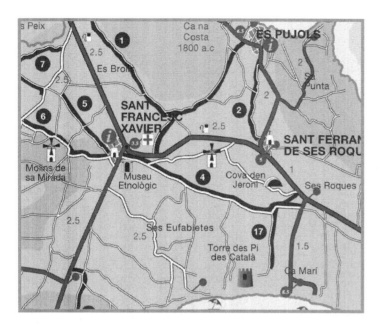

This is the scenic route between Sant Francesc and Sant Ferran. To get onto the route from Sant Francesc you enter the village via the main street off the main roundabout and take the first small street on the left.

Just Inside Route No.4

The route covers some beautiful farmland, and some nice fincas. Actually one of my favourite houses on the island is on the left hand side just a few hundred meters into to the route, and well worth pausing to admire:

Beautiful Finca on Route No.4

As you come to the end of the route (assuming you are heading towards Sant Ferran) you can either turn right onto Route No.17 and head down to the sea, or continue to a main road (Can Xumeu Ferrer) and turn left, which will bring to a junction connecting with the PM-820. Route No. 4 overshoots Sant Ferran by around a kilometre, so if that is your destination it is five minutes away by bicycle.

Another thing to keep an eye out for on the route is the office of a local architect. It is an incongruous design in the midst of rustic farmland, and it certainly stands out! I am a big fan of this type of architecture, but don't think it really fits with this landscape. I guess the fact that they managed to get it built is a testament to this architect's ability to navigate the Spanish planning process for its clients.

The Architect in Town

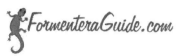

5.5. No.5: Cami de Porto-Sale

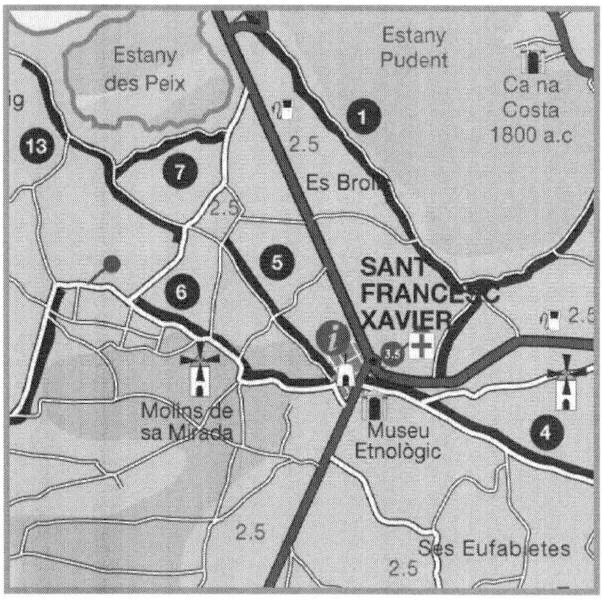

This is one of those frustrating routes that doesn't have a sign showing you where is starts. If you have the Eroski supermarket on your right, then keep cycling away from it and follow the road left until you get to the point below (you'll know it when you see it!), and turn right. If you see a large telecommunications tower you are heading in the right direction.

The right turn...

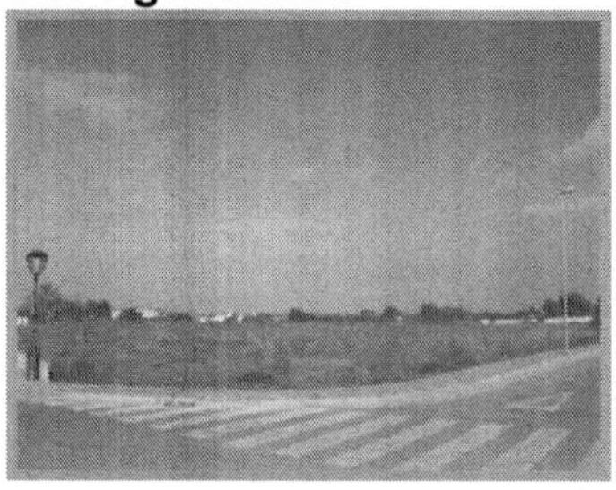

past some tennis courts...

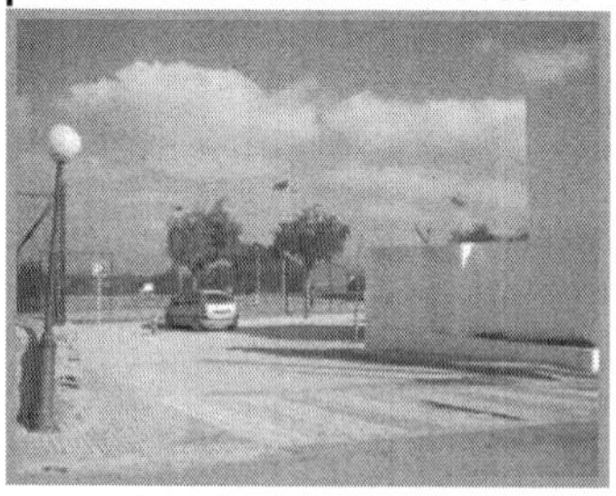

the route.

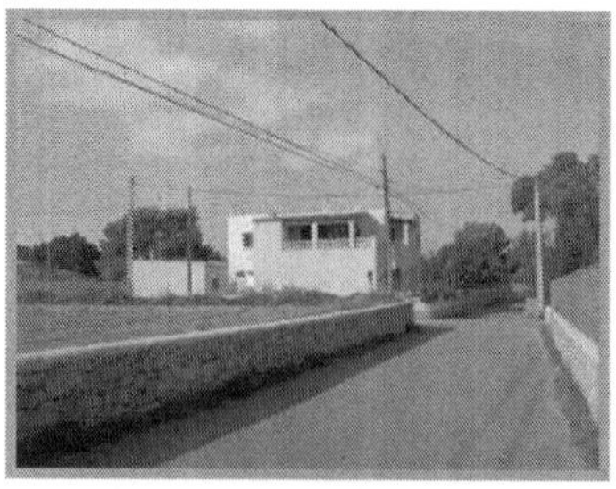

It's an easy tarmac route through farmland that comes to an abrupt end giving you three options: 1. turn left to connect to Estany des Peix 2. go straight down a rough farmland road to connect you to a different point on the Estany des Peix route. 3. turn right and cycle past the entrance to Estany des Peix and reach the PM-820, where you can turn left to La Savina, and right to Sant Francesc. If you are heading to Can Marroig take Option 1.

5.6. No.6: Cami de Dalt de Porto-Sale

(For map see route No.5 above)

Hiding around the corner from this white corrugated Gymnasium…

… is another poorly signposted, but charming route

The best way to get to this route is to take the road next to Bar Centro and head straight until the first right turn. The route is on the left just past the gymnasium. This is the road to Es Molins sa Mirada.

If you are not familiar with Bar Centro then you should become so right away. It's the very friendly café in Sant Francesc's main square.

The windmills are the feature of this route

5.7.   No.7: Cami de s'Estany des Peix

(For map see route No.5 above)

I am a big fan of the smaller of Formentera's two inland salt lakes, Estany des Peix, and combining Route No.7 with Route No.13 you can cycle around it. The entrance is just one kilometre outside la Savina, and its shallow waters, with small boats bobbing up and down, make it a very relaxing spot. It's another decent bird watching area, with plenty of terns and ducks.

The waters also have healing properties, well in a way at least. The new drug Yondelis is a marine derived anti-tumour agent. It is based on an extract of Estany des Peix's tunicate, and is now being produced synthetically for the treatment of patients with advanced soft tissue sarcoma.

Views of Ibiza Across Estany des Peix

5.8. No.8: Cami de ses Arenals

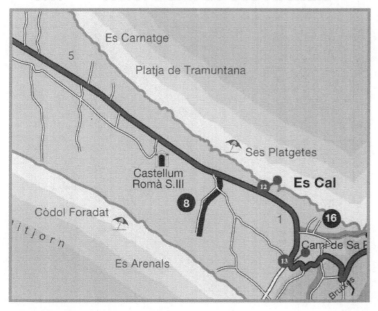

Ses Arenals is one of Mitjorn's most popular beaches, and is easily accessed via this turn off from the PM-820.

Turn left to keep on Route No.8...

...and you won't regret it!

5.9. No.9: Cami de sa Talaiassa

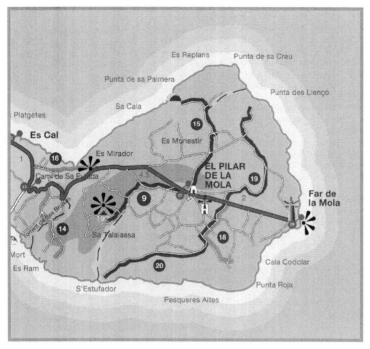

This is the first of the El Pilar routes and it takes you to a higher elevation than Es Mirador. Although you can see across the island's isthmus, the view is obscured by dense pine trees, thus the view from Route No. 16 is superior.

Although I wouldn't recommend this course for the view, it does make for great biking, and if you are leaving El Pilar it is a nice detour. You take a left to get onto the route just before you leave the village, and you can cut back down onto the PM-820 after checking out the view of the island.

**Turn left into here before leaving
The village of El Pilar.**

Scenes from the route.

5.10.   No.10: Cami de Cala Saona

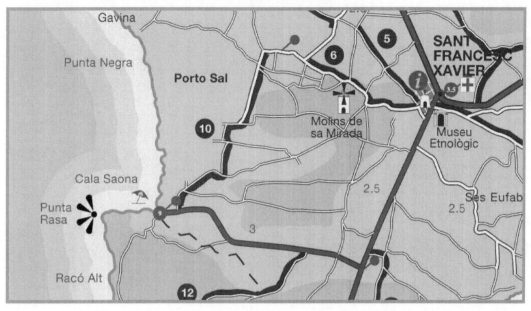

There are no signs at the entrance to this route. It leads you down a rugged road, into some of the most picturesque farmlands you will see. At the end of it all you get to the cove of Cala Saona, where you can take a dip, or hike on up to Punta Rasa if you have the energy. This is the best route to Cala Saona.

A Rugged Route

For Punta de la Gavina you would turn right at the sign on page 60 and follow the Cami de Dalt de Porto Sale, but to get onto Route 10 you go straight.

This sign reads, 'Cami de Dalt de Porto Sale'

5.11. No.11: Cami de Can Parra

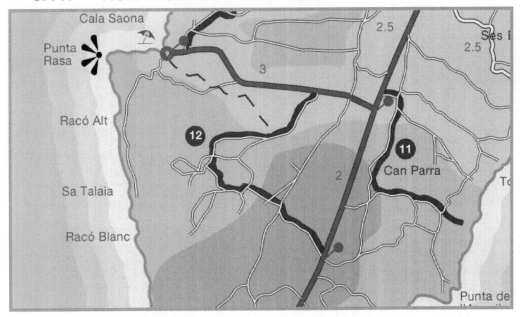

This is one of my favourite cycling paths on the island. It takes you through some winding country lanes to a beautiful view. It's easy to find this one – just zip through Sant Francesc, head south, and take the left at the first main junction.

When you get to the end of the route, you will come across a wall that points you in the direction of the beach. You need to park your bike and hike from this point. The wall has 'no entrada' painted on it, but this just means that you cannot go over the wall; it is perfectly fine to walk alongside it, and down to the views.

Route Entry Point

Ignore 'No Entrada' and follow the arrow.

It's well worth it!

I don't think housing gets much more basic than the finca below. Keep an eye out for it on Route 11.

Finca

5.12.   No.12: Cami des Cap

(For map see route No.11 above)

If you are going to take Route No. 12 then I bid you good luck, and ask that you send me your report if you make it back! This is not a route that is difficult to find the entrance to, but it is one where the exit can prove elusive. It has fantastic farmland that is reminiscent of a James Herriot novel, but the poor signposting can leave you as stranded as a cow birthing a calf without a vet. Sometimes the route is blocked, and you need to take a detour so don't expect to be able to follow the route as it is recorded on the map, but if exploring farmland is your thing, then you'll get to see some of the scenes below.

A Blocked Route. Time for a Detour

The Formentera Dales

5.13.   No.13: Cami de sa Pedrera

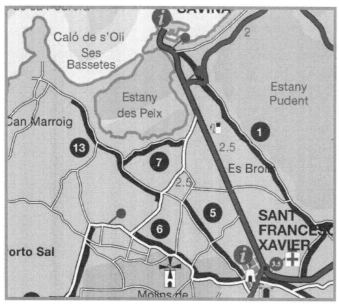

Linking up with Route No.7 this route will take you around the Estany des Peix salt lake, and on up to Can Marroig. It's a slightly bumpy ride, but is a relaxing one that also affords some decent bird watching opportunities. At the end of the route you will come across a designated picnic area tucked away inside a pine forest. There are a few nice houses along the way, many of which are French-owned.

Views, wetlands, and small boats.

5.14. No.14: Cami des Ram

(For map see route No.9 above)

First you will need some serious energy to cycle halfway up the incline to El Pilar de la Mola, next you will need some strong tires as you head down a rocky path to Es Ram, and finally you will need to keep some energy in reserve to make it back up to the top! By the relaxed standards of Formentera cycling it's one of the toughest routes, but it's nothing that can't be handled with a rental bike, and you can get off and walk any time. The entrance is not signposted, but you head on past the entrance to Hotel Riu, and turn right at the bins (see below).

Route Entrance

Route Path

Es Ram Cliffs

Views Out from Es Ram

5.15.   No.15: Cami de sa Cala

(For map see route No.9 above)

Congratulations, you made it up the hill to El Pilar, and are now ready for a countryside cycle. Route 15 is a good option, but first you need to find the entrance. As you come into town you will see the picturesque restaurant Taberna Can Blaiet La Mola. Turn left just before the restaurant, and you are on the right path. There is a gate along the way that you need to open to continue. There are no signposts so I have the photo below so you don't have to ask the way at a nearby farm like I did. Don't forget to shut the gate behind you.

Over the Fence

Route to the Sea

5.16. No.16: Cami de sa Pujada

(For map see route No.9 above)

At the 12.4km point of the PM-820 there is a turning into Cami de sa Pujada (it is on the left if you are heading into El Pilar). This track goes along the cliffs and gives you some great views out across the island's isthmus and over to Isla de S'Espardell.

Even though it is called the Roman Way (Cami Roma) it is unknown whether Romans actually used the path. It was used by Augustinian monks who named it after their founder, Sant Agusti, and climbed this path to reach their monastery in El Pilar de la Mola.

After undergoing a number of repairs the road does not look so Roman these days. In 1797 the Improvement Board commissioned an engineer named Pedro Groillez to repair the path, and in 2001 further repairs were undertaken.

Cami Roma, can only be walked, although some people push their bikes up so that they can zip down the highway once they reach the top. I'd recommend leaving your bikes at the bottom so you can enjoy the walk, and then just enjoy it again as you walk back down! Or you can hop on a bus. One thing I wouldn't do is walk the winding highway back down, as the cars are fast and there are seldom views through the pine trees.

One option is to take a break at the Es Mirador restaurant once you get to the top of the path. To get there you would turn right and walk a little way down the highway. Make sure you book ahead though as a lot of people have the same idea.

Entrance

Rock Formation on Pathway

Cove Views

The View from Es Mirador

5.17.   No.17: Cami de Can Simonet

(For map see route No.4 above)

I know this route well because I lived just behind it for a few months. It's a nice fork off Route No.4 and down to the water. Once you get to the sea below you can cycle across the beach, turn right at the defence tower, and take that road back to connect to Route No. 4. The short cycle along the shore is my favourite part of the journey.

Do not take the road on the right that the sign is pointing to. The entrance is a 150m further up on the left.

Not a bad cycle track, even with the clouds!

5.18.   No. 18 Cami d'es Torrent Fondo & No.20 Cami de s'Estufador

(For map see route No.9 above)

You will need a decent mountain bike for this route. A good quality rental will be fine, but don't expect a comfy ride. Once you get to the end of the route you will come across some houses. Given the paths that it has taken you to get there I am sure that you will be surprised that anyone sets up home here, even with those sea views.

One of the Better Paths

Looking Out to Far de la Mola

5.19.　No. 19 Cami d'es Monestir

(For map see route No.9 above)

This is a rural cycle, and if you are just up on Mola for the day I would recommend Routes 9,15, 18 and 20 as superior.

Farmland Route

6. Nature

6.1. Lizards

Over 2,000 years ago Formentera was recorded as the island of reptiles by Greek geographer Strabo, and today the lizard remains its symbol. The only lizard native to the island is *Podarcis pityusensis*, a species of lizard in the Lacertidae family, which is commonly known as the Ibiza Wall Lizard, the Pitiusan lizard, or Sargantana.

There over thirty different sub-species, including *P. pityusensis formenterae*, and you will notice different features on the lizards depending which part of the island they are from. For example, the lizards of La Mola are large and blue-green, whereas the lizards of Can Marroig are thinner and brown-grey. The islets around the Balearics also have separate sub-species of the lizard, for example, the blue lizard of Murada Island, and the bright green ones of S'Espartar.

The lizards live between the rocks that make up the farmland walls, in any sort of plantations or shrub land, and along rocky shores. They can also be found dwelling in arable land and urban areas. The males are slightly larger than the females, and the lizard feeds on insects and plants.

Spain's Ministry for the Environment monitors all the populations of the lizard on 70 islets and small islands around Ibiza and Formentera. Some species have already become extinct as a result of mixing (*P.p. miguelensis, P.p. subformenterae, P.p. algae, P.p. sabinae* and *P.p. grueni*), and this along with human encroachment is a pressure on population growth.

Two further types of geckos have been identified on the island (Tarentola mauritanica and Hemidactylus turcicus), but these were introduced by man.

The Symbol of Formentera

6.2. Loggerhead Turtles

There is a small population of loggerhead turtles (Caretta caretta) off the coast of Formentera. They are a protected species so you should not touch them, and if you see any wounded turtles it should be reported to the Centro de Recuperacion on 971 322 105.

6.3. Flora and Fauna

Formentera's soil consists mainly of sand and limestone which does not retain the water. This high permeability combined with low rainfall makes it an unforgiving place for plants, but there are some hardy species that thrive here. There are a variety of conditions in different places on the island, including desert-like, dunes, and wetlands.

Desert-Like

Some of the plants that you will see growing, even in the desolate plateaus of La Mola and Far de Barbaria are: Pistacia Lentiscus (evergreen shrub), Rosmarinus Officinalis (rosemary), Coridothymus Capitatus (thyme), Olea Europea (ollastre), Juniperus Oxycedrus (juniper), and Cistus Albidus (white rockrose).

Dunes

Survival in dune areas of the Mediterranean coast is only possible for plants that are able to cope with the conditions of unstable soil, strong salty winds and long dry seasons. The five plants below are examples of this, and they are commonly known as: 1. Sea daffodil 2. Silene 3. Broomlike 4. Marram Grass 5. Sea Lavender 6. Phoenician Juniper

Formentera's Coastal Fauna

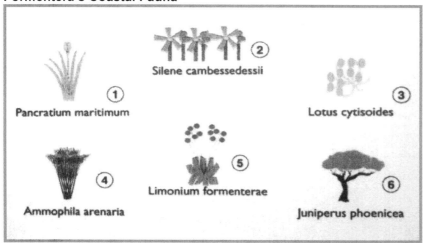

Up at Es Trucadors there is a plant which grows in the shallow waters separating Formentera from Espalmador, known as herba des Trucadors. It is said to relieve stomach aches.

Wetlands

In the wetlands around Estany Pudent and Estany des Peix a different range of flowers is to be found and these include: Silene cambessedessii, Diplotaxis ibicensis, Limonium gibertii, Limonium scorpiodesm, Limonium wiedmaninii, Limonium formenterae, and Limonium retusum.

Trees

As you would expect from one of the Pine Islands, there are plenty of pines trees around. Pinus halepensis, Pinus Pinea, and Juniperus sabina are some of the common varieties, and some of the most impressive pine forests surround the route up to El Pilar de la Mola.

Other trees include Opuntia Ficus-indica. This prickly pear cactus tree is seen many gardens as it provides food for livestock and is thought to prevent mosquitoes.

Dry fruit trees, such as the fig tree Ficus Carica, are also a common site. It is one of the most cultivated crops and you can spot them from their bent trunks, which are often supported by stakes.

The Prickly Pear

Posidonia
Beneath the sea are acres of posidonia beds. They play an essential part in balancing the Mediterranean ecosystem because of the amount of oxygen they produce and the fact that they act as a barrier to coastal erosion. Posidonia oceanica is one of nine species of posidonia, and it produces free floating fruit which are known in Italy as the olive of the sea. In 1999 UNESCO declared Formentera's posidonia beds as part of a world heritage site, and they are considered to be some of the best in the Mediterranean.

7. Practical Guide

In addition to the following section, the web site maintains the latest listings for restaurants, hotels etc. www.formenteraguide.com/directory

7.1.   Getting There

Unless you manage to book one of the limited helipad spots to get to the island, then you will be arriving by boat. In the summer they run from mainland Spain (Denia, Barcelona, Valencia) and from the Balearics (Palma, Eivissa). Most boats call in at Eivissa so the final leg of your journey will be the 30 minute ferry from Eivissa to Formentera.

Boat Companies
Acciona Transmediterránea
902 45 46 45
www.transmediterranea.es

Balearia
902 160 180 - 971 312 071
www.balearia.net

Iscomar
902 119 128
www.iscomar.es

Mediterránea - Pitiusa
971 322 443
www.medpitiusa.net

7.2. Emergency Directory

Emergency services are reached by dialling 112, and help is available in English, Spanish, Catalan and German.

Municipality:	971 32 10 87
Local Police:	092/ 971 32 20 87
Civil Guard:	971 32 20 22
Fireman:	092/112
Hospital:	971 32 12 12
Pharmacy, Sant Francesc:	971 32 24 19
Pharmacy, Es Pujols:	971 32 86 63
Pharmacy, Sant Ferran:	971 32 80 04
Taxis:	971 32 23 42

7.3.   Travel Agencies

Central de Viajes Formentera
av. de Joan Castelló i Guash,
29 - San Ferran.
tel. 971 321998 /99
fax. 971 321802
reservas@formenterafreetime.com

Es Freus
c/. de Sant Joan, Cantonada
8 d'Agost - San Francesc.
tel. 971 322284 /85
fax. 971 322471
esfreusformentera@contec.es

Primera Travel
edif. Auba, Local 1
c/. Almadraba - La Savina
tel. 971 322623
fax. 971 322706

Islamar
c/. de Santa Maria, s/n
Sant Francesc
tel. 971 322461
fax. 971 322011
islamar@interbook.net

TUI
av. Mediterráneo, 13
Puerto La Savina
tel. 971 322960
fax. 971 322289

7.4.   Transport

The best way to see the island is by bicycle as you get to cycle through dunes, along the coast, and across farmland. However, all modes of transport are available for hire, even quad bikes and electric cars.

The circuit bus travels from Far de la Mola to El Pilar, Mirador, and Sant Ferran. From Sant Ferran it loops around Estany Pudent via Es Pujols, Illetes, Port de la Savina and Sant Francesc. The route is divided into a short circuit for €6 which covers Port de la Savina, Illetes and Es Pujols, and the long circuit for €10 which covers all the stops. Between May and October the bus runs the loop between La Savina, Es Pujols, Sant Ferran and Sant Francesc every two hours.

Circuit Bus Route

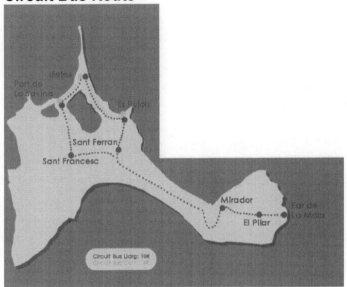

Car Rental
Avis: La Savina
tel. +34 971 32 10 13

Autos Es Caló: Es Caló
tel. +34 971 32 70 42

Autos Ca Marí: playa Migjorn
tel. +34 971 32 88 55

Autos Formentera: S.Francesc
tel. +34 971 32 28 17

Autos Isla Blanca Formentera: La Savina
tel. +34 971 32 25 59

Autos la Laguna: Es Pujols
tel. +34 971 328 492

Autos San Fernando: LaSavina
tel. +34 971 322 695

Betacar: La Savina
tel. +34 971 328 67

Formentera Autos: La Savina
tel. +34 971 321 049

Proauto: La Savina
tel. +34 971 323 226

Mopeds and Bikes
Formotor Rent: La Savina
tel. + 34 971 32 29 29

Moto Rent Mitjorn: La Savina
tel. +34 971 32 86 11

Moto Rent Pujols: Es Pujols
tel. +34 971 32 80 20

Moto Rent Reyes: Almadrava
tel. +34 971 32 33 37

Moto La Mola: Es Calo
tel. +34 971 32 70 22

La Savina Motos: La Savina
tel. +34 971 322 745

Moto Rent Mirada: Es Pujols
tel + 34 971 328888

Electrical Vehicle
Elektracar: La Savina
tel. +34 971 32 28 75

7.5.   Shopping

Shop opening times are generally from 9am to 2pm and from 5pm to 8pm. Some of the best shopping items on Formentera are made by contemporary artists living on the island. There are hippy markets, such as the one in Sant Francesc on Saturday mornings, and there is the art and crafts fair in Pilar de la Mola which runs on Wednesdays and Sundays from May to September.

The Hippy Heritage – an Es Pujols Shop

7.6.   Food and Drink

As an island Formentera has traditionally made use of local produce in its cooking rather than rely on expensive imports. For this reason the local dishes tend to be simple, with soups and stews that have a lot of local fish in them. Olives, figs, salt, and the local livestock are also key ingredients.

Lunch, la comida, is eaten at around 2pm, and dinner not until 10pm. You will find a few bars and restaurants that stay open through the siesta, and during the summer season most bars are open until 2am, with some remaining open until 6am. The menus are usually available in English, and have a lot of options.

Starters are varied, and some typical examples include: rice with sardines and cauliflower, rice with snails, noodles with rabbit, hotpot and gilthead soup. One of the most basic, that you will find at many restaurants, is a broad bean stew. This is made with broad beans, green beans, onions, tomatoes, garlic, sobrassada, bacon, paprika, vinegar, oil and salt. There is also a variation on this dish, fava pelada, which has noodles and chopped mint added.

Tapas

Local Pastries

Some of the typical fish dishes are squid stew with raisins and pine nuts, dogfish meatballs and plain old fish stew. One of my favourites is fisherman's hake, which is really all about getting the hake cooked to just the right level. The hake is sliced and served on top of a dish made from ripe tomatoes, potatoes, onion, garlic, parsley, paprika, salt, pepper and oil. There is also the all important sauce, and the ingredients vary from restaurant to restaurant, but it usually has lemon juice, olive oil and paprika.

Meat dishes include stuffed leg of lamb, baked pork with milk mushrooms and lamb stew with artichokes. Rabbit with peas is also a good option. The trick to this dish is to let the rabbit marinade overnight with lemon juice, salt and pepper. Some chefs like to use matured wine, but I find that this can dominate the taste. Sausage, peas, broad beans, onions and potatoes usually accompany this dish.

Cheese made from sheep and goat's milk is a specialty of food in Ibiza and Formentera, and there is a full range from mild to mature. There is also cow's milk cheese which is made with paprika, and this gives the rind a red tinge. In addition to the cheeses, there is a wide variety of prepared meats, including those making use of poultry, rabbit and lamb, the most common are: sobrassada (cured meat), botifarra (sausage), botifarro (black pudding), and ventre farcit (stuffed pork belly). The local rabbits are also well used in stews and casseroles. Usually these consist of a good fried sauce base, a spicy sauce, with fried rabbit liver, and are served with peas and

potatoes. Chicken is also a very common choice of meat in the stews and casseroles of Formentera.

7.7.   Restaurants

Rather can give an extensive ranking of restaurants I have reviewed a few in each village and encourage you to explore while you are there, and share your comments on our web site: http://www.formenteraguide.com/restaurants-formentera/

Café de Lago, La Savina
It has a good chef who makes nice salads and pizzas. It's popular with Italian footballers and looks out over a salt water lagoon.

Meditteraneo, La Savina
It's a bit pricy, but has great fish. It's quite an elegant place with a good view out to the sea.

El Sueno, Porto Saler
This is reservations only. It is international cuisine done very well and is only open for dinner.

Can Carlos, Sant Ferran
Dinner only. Reservations required. This is a great spot for a romantic al fresco dinner. It serves international cuisine with a tendency towards Italian.

Pivi, Sant Ferran
This is the place to come for local food. It's economical, has nice surroundings and does a good paella.

Capri, Es Pujols
Owned by a group of fishermen this serves up freshly caught fish in a garden surrounding. A simple, tasty menu.

Voramar, Es Pujols
Owned by the same group as Capri, but distinguished by having a fancier interior.

Pizza Pazza, Es Pujols
Good quality, local pizza.

Caminito, Es Pujols
Caminito is just outside Es Pujols at the entrance to Estany Pudent. With a massive iron billboard on its roof showing a couple dancing you can't miss it. As tacky as it may look from outside this Argentine steakhouse has some pretty special beef and great terraces around a pool. It doesn't serve lunch so make this an evening out.

Sa Varadero, Es Pujols
This place serves fish and meat, with the steaks done on an outdoor grill. It's only open in the evening and you will require a reservation. The place to be is on the terrace upstairs overlooking the Es Pujols beach.

Can Vent, Es Pujols
A lounge bar with a great cocktail list. They do superb ice creams too. You can stay there all day and enjoy breakfast, lunch and dinner.

Can Rafalet, Es Calo
A fish specialist that does a magnificent paella. During the day it is a great place for coffee and snacks. You will need to make a reservation.

Pascual, Es Calo
No terrace, but a well run fish restaurant.

Pequena Isla, El Pilar
A family-run restaurant with very high quality local and international dishes. It is popular with the locals and has great hams and rice dishes.

El Mirador, El Pilar
With the views from El Mirador the food is not the priority, but in fact it isn't too bad. Like a lot of the local restaurants it has paella, grilled fish and rice-based dishes. This place definitely requires a reservation, and it you are going to walk Cami Roma then this is the perfect place to take a rest afterwards.

Can Forn, Sant Ferran
This is a family-run place that specializes in tapas. It has good house wine and reasonable prices.

Bar Verdera, Sant Ferran
This is a meeting point for the locals and tourists alike. This is a place to sample some authentic tapas.

Macondo, Sant Ferran
This pizzeria is probably the best pizza on the island so make sure you go early

7.8.   Activities

7.8.1. Bird Watching

There are some excellent opportunities for bird watching on the island as species migrating from North Africa take a break. These include the woodchat, shrike, nightingale, and spotted flycatcher. The wetlands around Estany Pudent and Estany des Peix are also a rich breeding ground for local birds. All together there are over 200 species to look out for:

Audouin's Gull, Balearic Shearwater, Balearic Warbler, Barred Warbler, Blackcap, Black-headed Gull, Black-necked Grebe, Black-winged Stilt, Blue Rock-thrush, Bluethroat, Cattle Egret, Chaffinch, Common Moorhen, Common Shellduck, Common Starling, Common swift, Common Whitethroat, Corn Bunting, Cory's Shearwater, Crag Martin, Dartford Warbler, Eleonora's Falcon, Garden Warbler, Goldfinch, Grater Flamingo, Green Sandpiper, Greenshank, Grey Wagtail, Hoopoe, House Martin, House sparrow, Kentish Plover, Kingfisher, Linnet, Little Egret, Marsh Harrier, Meadow Pipit, Nightjar, Ortolan Bunting, Peregrine, Pied Avocet, Puffin, Razorbill, Redshank, Reed Warbler, Rock Sparrow, Ruff, Sardinian Warbler, Short-toed Lark, Skylark, Sparrow-hawk, Spectacled Warbler, Spotted Crake, Spotted Redshank, Stone Curlew, Storm Petrel, Thekla's Lark, Turnstone, Turtle Dove, Western Subalpine Warbler, Whinchat, White Wagtail, Woodchat Shrike, Yellow Wagtail

Some specific areas for ornithologists to visit are:

- The rocks and rosemary bushes are a breeding ground for the red-legged partridge, Thekla lark and rock thrush
- Peregrine falcons, Balearic shearwaters, and Audouin's gull are native to Formentera and can be spotted out on the island's many headlands
- The island of Espardell just off the northern tip has a colony of cormorants
- The adventurous bird watcher will move off land into Es Freus to look for storm petrel, the Balearic shearwater, fisher eagles, cormorants, yellow-legged gull, and Audouin's gull
- Out at Far de la Mola peregrine falcons nest in the cliffs, and the rock sparrows also take to the barren terrain.
- Over in Far de Barbaria you can find shearwaters, peregrine falcons, and gulls.

For further information see: www.formenterabirding.com

7.9.   Sailing

Sailing around Formentera has some favourable conditions for beginners, and enough challenging areas to satisfy Olympians such as Teresa Zabell who uses the island as a training base. Summer winds average between 5 and 15 knots. The winter can see storms of up to 30 knots. The prevailing winds come from the east in the summer, and the west in the winter.

Most boats approach via the North-West through the straits of Ses Portes, then thread between Illa des Penjats and an islet names Des Porcs, which has a lighthouse. Finally they pass Espalmador, and Formentera's northern peninsula of Es Trucadors before reaching Port de la Savina.

A sailboat can travel from the north to the south of the island in two hours, or head over to Ibiza in about the same time (the ferries take 30 minutes). As you sail around the island's 82km of coastline the cliffs, beaches and blue waters provide some variety in the landscape.

A popular spot for sailing is the northern peninsula, Es Trucadors, as it has something for everyone. It is a 3km beach running north to south with water on both sides. In the summer the eastern side has waves, whereas the western side has a calm sea. The conditions for sailing get rougher when you sail north or south of the peninsula by two miles.

Anchoring

If you sail to Formentera then you must observe its rules for anchoring. These are quite strict as the island protects its posidonia beds. The different types of anchoring zone that have been established are: free anchoring areas, regulated mooring areas with buoys, and restricted anchoring areas. The free anchoring areas have no limits to anchoring other than a maximum number of boats permitted in some areas. The regulated mooring areas with buoys have a number of regulations around their use, including a booking requirement. In the restricted anchoring areas the posidonia beds are being protected and it is only permitted to anchor to sandbars.

In the following maps the yellow boundaries are regulated mooring areas with buoys, and the red line marks restricted anchoring areas.

Calo de s'Oli

Espalmador

Buoys
The designated buoys where you can anchor are in place between 1 June and 30 September, and if you are planning to use one then you need to book in advance at: http://www.balearslifeposidonia.eu or by contacting the Department for the Environment (Conselleria de Medi Ambient) reservation centre on 902 422 425. Reservations can be made 2 to 20 days in advance, by phone or online. There is a restriction of two consecutive nights in a calendar week, one buoy per vessel and anchoring between buoys is not permitted.

There are different types of buoys with the colours indicating the permitted vessel length. The maximum safe wind speed is also recorded, and the Department of the Environment states that it will not accept any liability in the event that these conditions are exceeded.

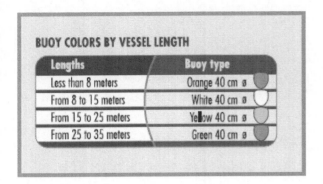

Lengths	Buoy type
Less than 8 meters	Orange 40 cm ø
From 8 to 15 meters	White 40 cm ø
From 15 to 25 meters	Yellow 40 cm ø
From 25 to 35 meters	Green 40 cm ø

A warden's boat patrols the area to check bookings, and is also on hand to give advice on the local conditions.

Warden's Craft

Aufsichtsboot mit den Kennzeichen der Balearischen Regierung

Warden's boat with Balearic Islands' Government markings

Anchoring Instructions

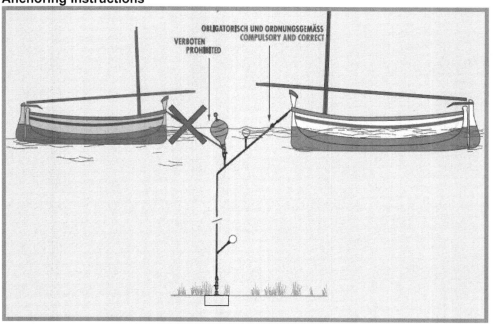

Mooring Point

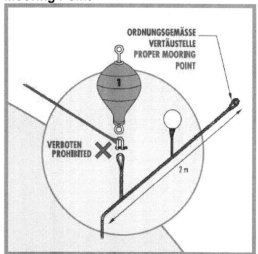

The most important rules to observe are to keep the length of the boat within the limits indicated by the colour of the buoy. Also, it is important not to moor two boats on the same buoy. At no time must you anchor on the posidonia, and you may only use sand banks when the buoys are occupied. If you do not take your buoy between 12.30 and 6.30pm of the arriving day then you may lose your reservation.

If would like to rent a boat or charter a cruise then one of the following companies will be able to help.

Sailing Schools & Charter Boats
Náutica Pins: La Savina
tel. 971 32 26 51

Barco Salao: La Savina
tel. 609 84 71 16

Fast Ferrari: La Savina
tel. 617 98 50 57

Formentera Rent a Boat: La Savina
tel. 971 32 10 89

Isla Azul: La Savina
tel. 971 32 34 24

7.10.   Diving

The clear waters of Formentera make them an excellent choice for diving, with very good visibility up to 50 meters in depth. In fact the Freus Marine Reserve of Ibiza and Formentera is the only natural area the Mediterranean Sea included on UNESCO's list of World Heritage Sites. You can dive year round with temperatures ranging from 15 degrees in the winter to 30 degrees in the summer.

Once you are under water there are a variety of landscapes to explore, from caves to shipwrecks, and acres of posidonia. You may even see a shark, as there have been basking sharks spotted off the coastline, and in 2008 an 18 footer was caught.

There are a number of protected species off the coast of Formentera, and you should refrain from disturbing them if you are lucky enough to spot one. Species to look out for are:

- Angel shark (squatina)
- Nursehound (scyliorhinus stellaris)
- Sting ray (dasyatis)
- Electric ray (torpedo)
- Great hammerhead shark (sphyrna)
- Blue shark (prionace glauca)
- Smooth hound (mustelus)
- Seahorse (hippocampus)
- Straightnose pipefish (nerophis ophidian)
- Sea crow (umbrina cirrosa umbrina cirrosa)

Diving Schools
Vellmari: Port La Savina
tel. 971 32 21 05
www.vellmari.com

Orca Sub: Hotel Formentera
Playa y Club Maryland
playa de Mitjorn
tel. 639 60 18 39
www.orcasub.com

Blue Adventure: Port La Savina
C/. Almadraba,67
tel. 971 32 11 68
www.blue-adventure.com

La Mola Diving: Hotel Riu la
Mola - playa Mitjorn
tel. 971 32 72 75
lamola@interbook.net

7.11. Water Sports

In addition to sailing and diving you can enjoy windsurfing, canoeing, jet-skis, water skiing, and parasailing on Formentera. On the beaches of Es Pujols and Illetes pretty much everything you need is available right there, and there are also rental stores across the island.

Rental Stores
Formentera Diving and Water Sports
Marina de la Savina, Formentera
Tel. 971 32 32 32

Escuela Municipal de vela: La Savina
tel. 667 56 13 50
www.4nomadas.com

Centro O'Neil: playa illetes
tel. 609 71 17 74

Barlovento: playa illetes
tel. 609 60 21 34

Wet 4 Fun: playa Es Pujols
tel. 670 36 63 14
www.wet4fun.com

7.11.1.   Festivals

Festa de Formentera is the main festival and takes place on the day of San Jaime, on the 25th July. The festivals have ancestral dances which are known as ball pages, where the women wear emprendada (jewellery made from brooches and pendants). The tabor, flute and castanets are the standard instruments.

Festivals

30 May: Sant Ferran celebrates the feast day of its patron saint
24 June: Midsummer solstice. This St. John's Day celebration is marked by a bonfire and fireworks in El Pilar
16 July: The feast of the Virgin del Carmen. If you head to La Savina you will see a maritime procession
25 July: Sant Jaume, the patron saint of Formentera, has his feast day marked by days of celebrations across the island
5 August: The patron saint of the Pine Islands, Virgin de les Neus, is commemorated
12 October: La Mola celebrates the Virgin del Pilar, on day that coincides with the first day of slaughtering the pigs
3 December: The feast day of Sant Francesc is the most traditional of the feast days, with many emprendada on show

National Holidays

-   1 January
-   6 January
-   Maundy Thursday
-   Good Friday
-   Easter Monday
-   1 May: the Day of Workers
-   15 August: the Assumption
-   12 October: the Virgin of Pilar
-   15 August: the Annunciation to Our Lady
-   1 November: All Saints Day
-   6 December: Spanish Constitution Day
-   8 December: Immaculate Conception of Our Lady
-   24 December: Christmas Eve
-   25 December: Nativity of Our Lord Jesus Christ
-   26 December: Saint Stephen's Day

7.12.   Real Estate

Many visitors to Formentera decide that they would like to purchase their own corner of paradise, but it is not easy. There is a very low stock of available housing, and the local population of around 7,000 are reluctant to sell. With strict restrictions on development and limited supply those that want to buy must set their criteria and play a waiting game for the right property to come onto the market. These conditions make the island expensive relative to the other Balearics, and the entry level price for a studio is around €250,000. For an extra €50,000 you might get a rural shack, but it is not until you have €800,000 or more to spend that you can expect a decent bit of land with some sea views. €4 million is the highest recorded sale on the island. There are houses worth more than that, however, they are not on the market. People build them to live in, not to sell.

Typical Farmhouse

Moroccan Influence

Traditional farm houses usually have one main rectangular room and a double sloping roof, known as es portxo, or sometimes a flat roof. Smaller rooms were added as needed so they can be ramshackle affairs.

A lot of the houses on the island are quite old so when you do get a place it might need a lot of work before it is your dream house. One thing that's quite common is for people to give the keys to an architect in September and then get them back in May along with a fully refurbished house. If you are going for a refurbishment then you may be interested to know that as of January 2010 there are only two heated swimming pools on the island. A heated pool that costs around €40,000 to install could put €100,000 of value onto the property and be a selling point.

When it comes to landscaping you need permission to cut trees, and the slow growing Sabina plant is protected. You can trim, and redirect their growth though. The best things for planting are succulent plants, geraniums, and tropical plants.

If you decide to build from scratch on the island then the local builders are best equipped to deal with simple designs. There are no strict design restrictions once you have the permission to build as long as you can demonstrate that the property will be environmentally friendly. From time to time you will see very modern designs in the midst of farmland.

One of the more distinctive architectural influences on the island was Henri Quilles who designed under the influence of Moroccan designs.

When evaluating properties it is important to consider access and utilities supply. You will notice that most of the roads are bumpy and the island wants to preserve them in this natural state so you are not permitted to tarmac roads. You can repair them with sand but this just washes away

anyway. A lot of residents like the fact that it is hard to get to their place because it stops tourists driving past to take a look, but you should bear in mind the type of car you will own/hire, and your willingness to navigate a narrow bumpy road.

Stone Kitchen Top

New House, Traditional Style

Some areas of the island do not have electricity and the properties run on generators and solar power. This can be fine in the summer, but if you are planning to stay year-round then this is not advisable. Also, if you are installing a swimming pool you will need to secure a certain capacity of electricity to have it heated. With regards to water, many houses run on cisterns which provide plenty of water, but not for drinking. If the water runs out you can easily get a delivery of water within hours to top you up.

The best thing to do if you are interested in buying a property is contact one of the local brokers such as Astbury (http://www.formentera-property.co.uk). They will be able to provide advice on all aspects of a purchase, from financing through to refurbishments. They are also letting agents so can help you get a yield on your property when you are not there.

8. Maps

The tourist office produces an excellent one page map for free that you can use to get around the island. It is reproduced below, but you should pick up a few A4 copies when you arrive at La Savina.

The local bookstores in Sant Francesc have a few more detailed maps available, but if you want some good English maps then it is best to buy them in advance. The Berlitz Holiday Map to Ibiza and Formentera is pretty good.

Northern Formentera

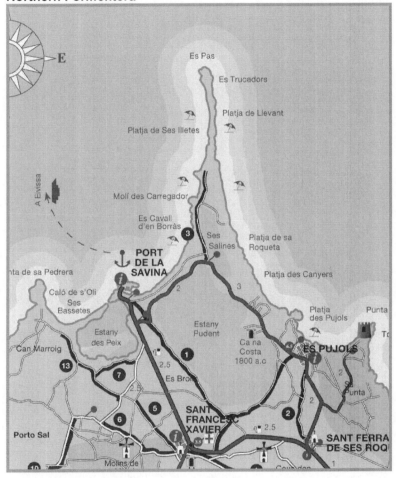

Southern Formentera

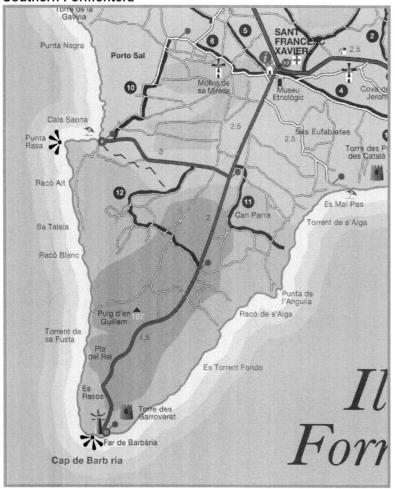

The Isthmus

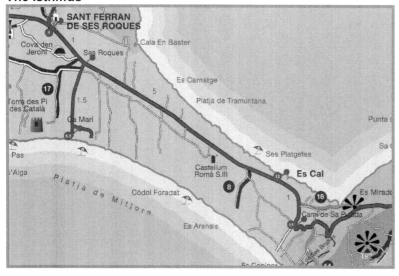

Eastern Formentera

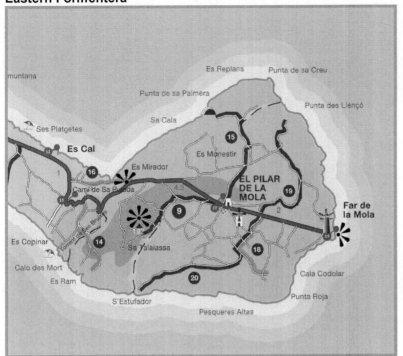

Printed in Great Britain by
Amazon.co.uk, Ltd.,
Marston Gate.